CAT
SELFIES

BY M.D. MULLINS

A POST HILL PRESS BOOK
ISBN: 978-1-64293-295-9

Post Hill Press
New York • Nashville
posthillpress.com

Published in the United States of America
Printed in Singapore
1 2 3 4 5 6 7 8 9 10

DEDICATION

To those who rescue, foster and adopt animals in need.
All cats featured were rescues. Many still need homes.

SPECIAL THANKS

REGINA CARRONE, Catopia Cat Rescue
KELLY PARKER, Chicago Cat Rescue
LANA VITSUP, Zani's Furry Friends
THERESA LABIANCA, Sean Casey Animal Rescue
ROBERTA GIORDANO, Bobbi and the Strays Pet Rescue
NORA WOOD & KITH BRADY, Anjellicle Cats Rescue
MARIA ROZOS & MICHELLE PORTLOCK, Infinite Hope
JENNILYN CARSON, East Harlem Kitty Rescue
EVA PROKOP & JENNA JANE MCMASTER, Whiskers-A-GoGo
SARA CAMERON & KEN SALERNO, Calling All Cats Rescue
MARIA CONLON, Give Me Shelter
LUSANA MASRUR, North Country Animal League
CATHERINE SNYDER, Second Chance Animal Center
DEBBIE EDGE & LISA BOURGAULT, Jake's Place Cat Rescue
JANE WARSHAW, Animal Welfare Warrior
LISA ALEXANDER, Animal Welfare Warrior
MARIA MILITO, Animal Welfare Warrior
SUSAN RICHARD, Animal Welfare Warrior
BUNNY HOFBERG, Animal Welfare Warrior
ESTHER KOSLOW, Animal Welfare Warrior

Smile, life is beautiful.

HAVING A CAT CAN
REDUCE YOUR RISK OF
HEART ATTACK OR
STROKE BY A THIRD.
STUDIES HAVE SHOWN
CAT COMPANIONSHIP
RELIEVES ANXIETY
AND STRESS.

Who do I gotta knead to

DID YOU KNOW

RESCUE ORGANIZATIONS
HAVE PARTNERED
WITH CORRECTIONAL
FACILITIES TO ALLOW
SELECT INMATES TO
FOSTER SHELTER CATS.
THE PROGRAMS ARE SAID TO
ALLEVIATE SHELTER
OVERCROWDING WHILE
HELPING TO REHABILITATE
THE INCARCERATED.

So, you're 40 and single?

DID YOU KNOW

WHILE CAT OWNERSHIP IS
TRADITIONALLY ASSOCIATED
WITH WOMEN, A NEW
STUDY FINDS THAT
AMONG MILLENNIALS
IN THE UNITED STATES,
MEN DOMINATE.

I didn't bring you bad luck.

DID YOU KNOW

IN CONTRAST TO THE
BACKWARD VIEW THAT
BLACK CATS ARE BAD LUCK,
IN ENGLAND THESE MINI
PANTHERS ARE ASSOCIATED
WITH GOOD FORTUNE.
ALSO, SAILORS HAVE
HISTORICALLY KEPT
BLACK CATS FOR
SAFE TRAVEL.

Pass the catnip.

DID YOU KNOW

ABOUT ONE THIRD OF
CATS HAVE NO REACTION
TO CATNIP.
THESE CATS LACK THE
GENE NECESSARY FOR
CATNIP STIMULATION.
KITTENS LESS THAN THREE
MONTHS OF AGE ALSO
DO NOT RESPOND
TO CATNIP.

I go into survival mode when tickled.

DID YOU KNOW

A THIRD OF THOSE BIT
BY A CAT IN THE
UNITED STATES REQUIRE
MEDICAL ATTENTION.
WHILE DOG BITES
ARE MORE COMMON,
CAT BITES CAN OFTEN
CAUSE INFECTION.

Lost my ears, retained my beauty.

DID YOU KNOW

A CAT'S EXTERNAL EAR
ROTATES UP TO 180 DEGREES
ALLOWING IT TO HEAR
THE FAINTEST OF SOUNDS.
CATS CAN ALSO HEAR AT
HIGHER FREQUENCIES
THAN DOGS.

So tell me again why

KITTY LITTER,
AS WE KNOW IT TODAY,
WAS INVENTED BY
ENTREPRENEUR
ED LOWE
IN 1947.
IT IS NOW A
$2 BILLION INDUSTRY

Nobody's perfect. But I'm close.

DID YOU KNOW

NEARLY ALL
TORTOISESHELL CATS
ARE FEMALE.
IN IRISH FOLKLORE
THEY BRING GOOD LUCK.

Fall asleep, I dare you.

DID YOU KNOW

DESPITE WHAT MANY
BELIEVE, CATS DO NOT
HOLD GRUDGES.
BAD BEHAVIOR IS
TYPICALLY A RESULT OF
STRESS THE CAT IS
FEELING AND NOT THEIR
DECISION TO
EXACT REVENGE,
BEHAVIORISTS CLAIM.

Wait, a bath involves water?

WHILE MANY CATS HAVE AN AVERSION TO WATER, CERTAIN BREEDS, SUCH AS THE TURKISH VAN, ARE KNOWN FOR HAVING AN H_2O AFFINITY AND HAVE BEEN NICKNAMED 'THE SWIMMING CATS.'

Tastes like chicken.

DID YOU KNOW

LINEAR FOREIGN BODIES, SUCH AS THREAD, STRING AND RIBBON, ARE THE MOST COMMON CAUSE OF INTESTINAL OBSTRUCTION IN CATS, AND CAN LEAD TO SERIOUS INTERNAL DAMAGE, EVEN DEATH. CATS MUST BE SUPERVISED WHEN PLAYING WITH SUCH MATERIALS.

My father was a werewolf.

DID YOU KNOW

A CALIFORNIA CAT
NAMED SOPHIE SMITH
HOLDS THE RECORD
FOR LONGEST HAIR
WITH A SINGLE
STRAND
MEASURING
JUST SHY OF 11 INCHES.

Mickey, you're mine.

DID YOU KNOW

A SINGLE CAT IS CREDITED
WITH HAVING KILLED
28,899 MICE.
THE CAT, NOT PICTURED,
WAS A LONG-HAIRED
TORTOISESHELL
NAMED TOWSER AND HER
DOMAIN WAS THE
GLENTURRET DISTILLERY
IN SCOTLAND.
SHE LIVED 24 YEARS.

Best friends always have your back.

DID YOU KNOW

A FEMALE KITTEN CAN
BECOME PREGNANT
AT 4 MONTHS OF AGE.
WITH GESTATION LASTING
63 TO 65 DAYS,
A KITTEN CAN HAVE
HER OWN LITTER
AT 6 MONTHS OF AGE.
IT'S IMPORTANT TO
SPAY AND NEUTER.

Is the bear still following me?

IT IS NOT UNCOMMON
FOR CATS TO FEAR
INANIMATE OBJECTS
THAT LACK FAMILIARITY.
AS FOR THOSE WHO
FEAR CATS, THEY SUFFER
FROM AILUROPHOBIA.

My wingman.

DID YOU KNOW

ATTACKS BY CATS
ARE AMONG THE
MOST COMMON CAUSE
OF BAT CASUALTIES.

You work 60 hours weekly, I sleep
16 hours daily. You own me?

DID YOU KNOW

CATS ON AVERAGE SLEEP
70% OF THE DAY
TO CONSERVE ENERGY.
HARDWIRED TO HUNT,
CATS IN THE WILD
REQUIRE EVERY BIT
OF ENERGY TO CATCH
THEIR PREY WHETHER THAT
BE A BIRD, MOUSE OR IN THIS
CASE, A FEATHER TEASER.

Have a seat, we were expecting you.

THE LENGTH OF A KITTEN'S WHISKERS AND THE WIDTH OF THEIR BODY ARE APPROXIMATELY EQUAL AS KITTENS OFTEN RELY ON THEIR WHISKERS TO NAVIGATE INITIALLY. SECURELY CONNECTED TO THE CAT'S NERVOUS SYSTEM, WHISKERS SHOULD NEVER BE CUT.

One eye. One heart. All yours.

DID YOU KNOW

CATS SMILE BY
SQUINTING AT US.
SLOW BLINKING,
HEAD-BUNTING AND
KNEADING ARE OTHER SIGNS
THAT YOUR CAT IS
CONTENT WITH YOU.
WHILE CATS CAN
SMILE, BEHAVIORISTS SAY
SUCH EXPRESSIONS ARE NOT
A SIGN OF AFFECTION.

Life is uncertain. Eat dessert first

DID YOU KNOW

CATS DO NOT
HAVE A SWEET TOOTH.
CATS LACK CERTAIN TASTE
RECEPTOR PROTEINS ON
THEIR TONGUE,
MAKING IT IMPOSSIBLE
FOR THEM TO TASTE SWEETS.
CATS ARE THE ONLY
KNOWN MAMMAL
UNABLE TO TASTE SWEETS.

Always bring your slay game.

DID YOU KNOW

MALE CATS CAN MOUNT
A FEMALE IN HEAT IN
AS LITTLE AS 16 SECONDS.
ON AVERAGE, MATING
CAN TAKE ANYWHERE
FROM ONE TO NINE MINUTES
AND ONCE COMPLETE,
THE MALE CAT
ABANDONS THE FEMALE.

Wanna hear a scary story?

DID YOU KNOW

IN JAPANESE FOLKLORE,
CATS CAN MORPH
INTO SUPERNATURAL,
BLOOD-THIRSTY CREATURES
KNOWN AS THE BAKENEKO
OR 'GHOST CAT.'
DESPITE THE INTENSE
STARE, THE CAT PICTURED
IS NOT A BAKENEKO
AND IS QUITE FRIENDLY.

Your tuna or your life.

TOO MUCH TUNA CAN
CAUSE MALNUTRITION
AND TOXICITY IN CATS.
TUNA LACKS THE
NUTRIENTS CATS REQUIRE
IN THEIR DIET AND
CAN LEAD TO
MERCURY POISONING.

Sassy, classy, and a bit bad-assy.

DID YOU KNOW

CATS MARK YOU AS
THEIR TERRITORY BY
RUBBING AGAINST
YOU WITH THEIR
SCENT GLANDS.
CONSIDER YOURSELF
LUCKY, CATS ALSO
USE URINE TO MARK
THEIR TERRITORY.

Let my eyes do the talking.

THE GLIMMER WE SEE
IN A CAT'S EYE AT NIGHT
IS A RAY OF SUNLIGHT
STORED FOR SAFEKEEPING
BY THE SUN GOD RA
'TIL DAY RETURNS,
SO SAY THE
ANCIENT EGYPTIANS.

This is me surprised.

DID YOU KNOW

300,000 MUMMIFIED CATS
WERE FOUND IN 1888
IN AN ANCIENT
EGYPTIAN CEMETERY.
THE CAT MUMMIES WERE
STRIPPED AND SOLD
AS FERTILIZER TO
FARMERS IN ENGLAND.

Pedicure time.

DID YOU KNOW

DECLAWING A CAT IS
AN AMPUTATION OF
THE CAT'S BONE
THAT CAN CAUSE LASTING
PHYSICAL PROBLEMS,
WHILE PROVIDING
NO MEDICAL BENEFIT.
INSTEAD, CATS SHOULD
HAVE THEIR NAILS
TRIMMED EVERY
2 TO 4 WEEKS.

Our ears light-up when we ignore you

DID YOU KNOW

APPROXIMATELY 80% OF
ORANGE TABBIES ARE MALE.
THE REASON:
FEMALE ORANGE TABBIES
REQUIRE BOTH PARENTS
TO HAVE AN ORANGE COAT
WHEREAS MALES ONLY NEED
THEIR MOTHER TO HAVE
THE ORANGE GENE.

Is the zombie apocalypse over?

DOMESTIC CATS
CAN REACH A SPEED OF
NEARLY 30 MPH
WITHIN SECONDS.
THE SPEED LASTS ONLY
IN SHORT SPURTS,
WHICH IS KEY
TO CATCHING PREY
AND
OUTRUNNING ZOMBIES.

Can I spend all 9 lives with you?

DID YOU KNOW

MORRIS THE CAT,
THE 9LIVES BRAND
OF CAT FOOD MASCOT,
WAS A RESCUE CAT
ADOPTED
FROM AN ILLINOIS
ANIMAL SHELTER.

I'm ready for my closeup.

MORE THAN
TWO-THIRDS OF
BLUE-EYED WHITE CATS
ARE DEAF IN AT
LEAST ONE EAR.
ABOUT 20% OF WHITE CATS
WITH NONBLUE EYES
ARE ALSO DEAF.

Cuddle time?

DID YOU KNOW

THE HORMONE OXYTOCIN
IS RELEASED WHEN ONE
STROKES A CAT.
THE SAME HORMONE
IS ALSO ASSOCIATED
WITH MATERNAL
ATTACHMENT
AND SEXUAL PLEASURE.

WARNING: You may fall in love with me.

DID YOU KNOW

OUTGOING CATS HAVE
A BETTER CHANCE
OF GETTING ADOPTED.
IN CONTRAST,
A DOG'S APPEARANCE,
MORE SO THAN
THEIR BEHAVIOR,
IS SAID TO PLAY A
GREATER ROLE IN ITS
ADOPTION.

It's not me. It's you.

DID YOU KNOW

CATS PERCEIVE HUMANS
TO BE BIG, DUMB CATS,
SO SAYS BRITISH
ANTHROZOOLOGIST
JOHN BRADSHAW,
WHO HAS BEEN STUDYING
CATS FOR 30 YEARS.

Give me a scotch, I am starving.

DID YOU KNOW

A TABLESPOON
OF ALCOHOL CAN PUT
A CAT IN A COMA.
CATS SHOULD NEVER
CONSUME ALCOHOL,
AS EXPOSURE HAS
RESULTED
IN BRAIN AND
LIVER DAMAGE,
AS WELL AS DEATH.

You talking to me?

DID YOU KNOW

DOMESTIC CATS
SHARE MORE THAN
95% OF THEIR DNA
WITH TIGERS.
HUMANS SHARE
ABOUT 90% OF THEIR
DNA WITH
DOMESTIC CATS.

I do a thing called what I want.

DID YOU KNOW

WHILE A CAT OFTEN RECOGNIZES THEIR OWNER'S VOICE, THEY TYPICALLY CHOOSE TO IGNORE IT. RESEARCHERS ATTRIBUTE THIS DISMISSIVENESS TO THEIR EVOLUTIONARY HISTORY.

First spa day.

DID YOU KNOW

THE MOST PROLIFIC CAT
ON RECORD WAS A
TABBY FROM TEXAS.
NAMED DUSTY,
SHE GAVE BIRTH TO
420 KITTENS
IN HER LIFETIME.
DUSTY'S FIRST LITTER
WAS IN JUNE OF 1952
AND CONSISTED OF JUST
ONE KITTEN.

Ever been devoured by a blanket?

DID YOU KNOW

MUCH LIKE
HUMAN FINGERPRINTS,
EACH CAT'S NOSE PRINT,
WITH ITS PATTERN OF
RIDGES AND BUMPS,
IS UNIQUE.

I taught Pele everything he knows.

DID YOU KNOW

AN ADOPTED CAT
NAMED DIDGA,
NOT PICTURED,
HOLDS THE
GUINNESS RECORD
FOR MOST TRICKS
PERFORMED IN A MINUTE.
FROM ROLLING OVER
TO SKATEBOARD JUMPING,
DIDGA PERFORMED
20 TRICKS IN 60 SECONDS.

Catnip every minute.

DID YOU KNOW

CATS SENSITIVE TO
THE EFFECTS OF CATNIP
MELLOW OUT WHEN
THEY INGEST THE HERB,
AND BECOME PLAYFUL
WHEN THEY SMELL IT.
FOR HUMANS, CATNIP
HAS A CALMING EFFECT.

You sleep on the floor tonight, human.

DID YOU KNOW

MORE THAN TWO-THIRDS
OF CAT OWNERS SLEEP
WITH THEIR CATS.
A STUDY FINDS THAT
62% OF ADULTS
SLEEP WITH THEIR CATS,
WHILE AN ADDITIONAL
13% OF CHILDREN
ALSO SLEEP WITH THEIR
FELINE COMPANIONS.

When does this story end?

DID YOU KNOW

THE SAME GENE
RESPONSIBLE FOR GIVING
THE CHEETAH IT'S SPOTS
GIVES THE TABBY
IT'S STRIPES.
IF THE GENE
IS MUTATED,
THE STRIPES WILL
APPEAR BLOTCHED
ON THE TABBY.

Kitten today. Panther tomorrow.

TWENTY-TWO CAT BREEDS
CAN HAVE
SOLID BLACK COATS.
WITH THE RARE EXCEPTION
OF A SABLE-COLORED KITTEN,
THE BOMBAY CAT
IS THE ONLY BREED THAT
IS EXCLUSIVELY BLACK.

We come in every flavor.

DID YOU KNOW

A SINGLE LITTER
OF KITTENS CAN HAVE
MULTIPLE FATHERS.
WHILE IN HEAT,
A FEMALE CAN MATE
WITH SEVERAL MALES,
RESULTING IN DIFFERENT
TOM CATS FERTILIZING
DIFFERENT EGGS.

Wake up mom. Wake up.

DID YOU KNOW

MOTHER CATS OFTEN
COMMUNICATE
WITH THEIR KITTENS
THROUGH A UNIQUE SOUND
KNOWN AS A CHIRRUP.
AS ADULTS,
CATS USE THE SAME SOUND
WITH HUMANS THEY
LOVE AND TRUST.

The best cats are a bit crazy.

DID YOU KNOW

A CONNECTICUT CAT
NAMED LEWIS WAS PLACED
UNDER HOUSE ARREST IN 2006.
THE SAME CAT HAD A
RESTRAINING ORDER
FILED AGAINST HIM
FOR ALLEGEDLY
ATTACKING LOCALS.
LEWIS, NOT PICTURED,
IS NOW AN INDOOR CAT.

If we fit, we sit.

DID YOU KNOW

CATS HAVE FREE-FLOATING
CLAVICLE BONES.
THIS ALLOWS THEM
TO FIT INTO THE
TIGHTEST OF SPACES
AND CONTORT
THEIR BODY
WITH EASE.

I'm Prada. You're Nada.

DID YOU KNOW

U.S. CONSUMERS
SPENT MORE THAN
$72 BILLION
ON THEIR PETS IN 2018.
IN 1994, U.S. CONSUMERS
SPENT $17 BILLION
ON THEIR PETS.

Don't swim with sharks.

When can we swim with more sharks?

PHOTO CREDIT INDEX

1.   Photo by Kelly Parker, Chicago Cat Rescue Volunteer Photographer (www.chicagocatrescue. org/) / (773) 203-0215

2.   Kate Devlin, 'Owning a cat 'cuts stroke risk by third,' The Telegraph, March 19 2008

3.   Photo by Lana Vitsup, Zani's Furry Friends Volunteer Web Master/Designer, Photographer, Writer, Instagram Manager (https://zanisfurryfriends.org/)

4.   Nicole Hamilton, 'Innovative prison program gives cats (and inmates) a bright future,' BestFriends.org, June 27 2016

5.   Photo by Kelly Parker, Chicago Cat Rescue Volunteer Photographer (www.chicagocatrescue. org/) / (773) 203-0215

6.   Statista.com, 'Cat and dog ownership among U.S. Millennials, by gender 2017' (www.statista. com/statistics/831452/pet-ownership-united-states-millennials-cat-dog/)

7.   Rescued/Adopted Bronx, NY Kitten

8.   Louise Hung, '7 Ways Black Cats Bring Good Luck Around the World,' Catster.com, October 29 2018

9.   Photo by Staff at North Country Animal League (www.ncal.com)

10.   Pam Johnson-Bennett, 'The Catnip Response,' CatBehaviorAssociates.com

11.   Photo by Lana Vitsup, Zani's Furry Friends Volunteer Web Master/Designer, Photographer, Writer, Instagram Manager (https://zanisfurryfriends.org/)

12.   'Is a Cat Bite Worse than a Dog Bite?' Animal Medical Center Blog, May 14 2014 (www. amcny.org/blog/2014/05/14/is-a-cat-bite-worse-than-a-dog-bite)

13.   Photo by Kelly Parker, Chicago Cat Rescue Volunteer Photographer (www.chicagocatrescue. org/) / (773) 203-0215

14.   Jane A. Kelley, '6 Cool Facts About Cat Ears' Catster.com, August 4 2017

15.   Photo by Lana Vitsup, Zani's Furry Friends Volunteer Web Master/Designer, Photographer, Writer, Instagram Manager (https://zanisfurryfriends.org/)

16.   Daniel A. Gross, 'How Kitty Litter went from happy accident to $2 billion industry,' The Washington Post, February 2 2015

17.   Photo by Lisa Bourgault of Fuzzball Photography, Jake's Place Cat Rescue (www. jakesplacecatrescue.org/)

18. Selena Barrientos, '10 Totally Fascinating Facts About Tortoiseshell Cats,' GoodHouseKeeping.com, June 4 2019

19. East Harlem Kitty Rescue / eastharlemkitty@aol.com

20. Marilyn Krieger, 'Your Cat Doesn't "Get Even" With You Through Unwanted Behavior,' Catster.com, March 20 2015

21. Infinite Hope (www.infinitehope.org) / infinitehopeanimalrescue@gmail.com

22. Laura Moss, '9 Cat Breeds That Love Water,' AdventureCats.org, October 19, 2015

23. Photo by Kelly Parker, Chicago Cat Rescue Volunteer Photographer (www.chicagocatrescue.org/) / (773) 203-0215

24. Arnold Plotnick DVM, 'Linear Foreign Bodies in Cats,' ManhattanCats.com

25. Whiskers-A-GoGo (www.whiskers-agogo.org) / whiskersagogo.nyc@gmail.com

26. 'Longest fur on a cat,' (www.guinnessworldrecords.com/world-records/longest-fur-on-a-cat)

27. Photo by Regina Carrone, Catopia Cat Rescue Director (catopiacatrescue.org) / catopiacatrescue@gmail.com

28. 'Greatest mouser' (www.guinnessworldrecords.com/world-records/greatest-mouser/)

29. Photo by Regina Carrone, Catopia Cat Rescue Director (catopiacatrescue.org) / catopiacatrescue@gmail.com

30. Amy Flowers DVM, 'What to Expect When Your Cat Is Pregnant,' Pets.WebMD.com, May 20 2019

31. Anjellicle Cats Rescue (www.AnjellicleCats.com) / info@anjelliclecats.com

32. Maura McAndrew, '8 Common Cat Fears and Anxieties' PetMD.com

33. Whiskers-A-GoGo (www.whiskers-agogo.org) / whiskersagogo.nyc@gmail.com

34. Bat Conservation Trust (www.bats.org.uk/about-bats/threats-to-bats/cat-attacks)

35. Photo by Bridgette Murray, Calling All Cats Rescues Volunteer / cacreventsmgr@gmail.com

36. Jawad Ahmad, 'Cats spend 70% of their lives asleep,' VeterinaryHub.com, June 13 2013

37. Photo by Lana Vitsup, Zani's Furry Friends Volunteer Web Master/Designer, Photographer, Writer, Instagram Manager (https://zanisfurryfriends.org/)

38. Yahaira Cespedes, 'Why Do Cats Have Whiskers?' PetMD.com

39. Photo by Michelle Portlock, Infinite Hope Board VP (www.infinitehope.org) / infinitehopeanimalrescue@gmail.com

40. Ingrid Newkirk, 'Reading Your Cat's Eyes,' PETA.org, September 13 2018 // Charlotte Corney, 'Can cats smile?' ScienceFocus.com

41. East Harlem Kitty Rescue / eastharlemkitty@aol.com

42. David Biello, 'Strange but True: Cats Cannot Taste Sweets,' ScientificAmerican.com, August 16 2007

43. Photo by Regina Carrone, Catopia Cat Rescue Director (catopiacatrescue.org) / catopiacatrescue@gmail.com

44. Beth Asaff, 'Male Cat Behavior Characteristics,' Cats.LoveToKnow.com

45. Anjellicle Cats Rescue (www.AnjellicleCats.com) / info@anjelliclecats.com

46. Alicia McDermott, 'Beware of the Cat: Tales of the Wicked Japanese Bakeneko and Nekomata,' Ancient-Origins.net, November 6 2015

47. Photo by Kelly Parker, Chicago Cat Rescue Volunteer Photographer (www.chicagocatrescue.org/) / (773) 203-0215

48. Amy Flowers, 'Foods Your Cat Should Never Eat,' Pets.WebMD.com, February 27 2018

49. Photo by Kelly Parker, Chicago Cat Rescue Volunteer Photographer (www.chicagocatrescue.org/) / (773) 203-0215

50. Samantha Drake, 'Cat Behavior: Why Do Cats Rub Against You?' PetMD.com

51. Photo by Scott Berliner, Sean Casey Animal Rescue (www.nyanimalrescue.org) / adopt@nyanimalrescue.org

52. Justine Hankins, 'Windows of a cat's soul,' TheGuardian.com, June 27 2003

53. Photo by Staff at North Country Animal League (www.ncal.com) / info@ncal.com

54. Beach Combing, 'Tens of Thousands of Egyptian Mummies in English Soil?' StrangeHistory.net, December 18 2013

55. Photo by Regina Carrone, Catopia Cat Rescue Director (catopiacatrescue.org) / catopiacatrescue@gmail.com

56. 'Declawing cats: Far worse than a manicure' (www.humanesociety.org/resources/declawing-cats-far-worse-manicure)

57. Photo by Rachel Baird, East Harlem Kitty Rescue / eastharlemkitty@aol.com

58. Susan Pi, 'Why Orange Cats Are Usually Male,' CatTime.com

59. Photo by Regina Carrone, Catopia Cat Rescue Director (catopiacatrescue.org) / catopiacatrescue@gmail.com

60. Cameron Stracher, 'Usain Bolt Versus the House Cat,' WSJ.com, August 23 2009

61. Bobbi and the Strays Pet Rescue (www.bobbiandthestrays.org) / info@bobbicares.org

62. 'Hinsdale Humane Society – Home of Morris the Cat,' (https://www.hinsdalehumanesociety.org/about/morris-the-cat)

63. Photo by Regina Carrone, Catopia Cat Rescue Director (catopiacatrescue.org) / catopiacatrescue@gmail.com

64. 'White Cats and Blindness/Deafness,' (https://www.vet.cornell.edu/departments-centers-and-institutes/cornell-feline-health-center/health-information/feline-health-topics/ask-elizabeth-white-cats-and-blindnessdeafness)

65. Photo by Lana Vitsup, Zani's Furry Friends Volunteer Web Master/Designer, Photographer, Writer, Instagram Manager (https://zanisfurryfriends.org/)

66. Tara Green, 'Do Cats Emit Something That Makes You Love Them?' Pets.TheNest.com // 'What Is Oxytocin?' (https://www.psychologytoday.com/us/basics/oxytocin)

67. Photo by Kelly Parker, Chicago Cat Rescue Volunteer Photographer (www.chicagocatrescue.org/) / (773) 203-0215

68. Shaunacy Ferro, '11 Surprising Facts About Cat Adoptions,' MentalFloss.com, June 6 2017

69. East Harlem Kitty Rescue / eastharlemkitty@aol.com

70. Chris Matyszczyk, 'Scientist: Cats think you are just a big, stupid cat,' CNET.com, January 12 2014

71. Photo by Regina Carrone, Catopia Cat Rescue Director (catopiacatrescue.org) / catopiacatrescue@gmail.com

72. 'Human Foods that are Dangerous for Cats,' (https://m.petmd.com/cat/emergency/poisoning-toxicity/c_ct_human_food_poisoning)

73. Photo by Lana Vitsup, Zani's Furry Friends Volunteer Web Master/Designer, Photographer, Writer, Instagram Manager (https://zanisfurryfriends.org/)

74. Tia Ghose, 'House cats and tigers share 95.6 percent of DNA, study reveals,' CSMonitor.com, September 18 2013 // Steven Silz-Carson, 'How much DNA do humans share with cats? What physical and psychological common features do they share?' Quora.com, January 11 2017

75. Photo by Lana Vitsup, Zani's Furry Friends Volunteer Web Master/Designer, Photographer, Writer, Instagram Manager (https://zanisfurryfriends.org/)

76. Rachel Nuwer, 'Cats Recognize Their Owner's Voice But Choose to Ignore It,' Smithsonian.com, December 2 2013

77. Photo by Theresa LaBianca, Sean Casey Animal Rescue (www.nyanimalrescue.org) / adopt@nyanimalrescue.org

78. 'Most prolific cat,' Guinness World Records (www.guinnessworldrecords.com/world-records/most-prolific-cat)

79. Photo by Santana Snyder, Second Chance Animal Rescue Feline Associate (2ndchanceanimalcenter.org) / felineoffice@2ndchanceanimalcenter.org

80. Jane A Kelley, '4 Cool Facts About Cat Noses,' Catster.com, August 9 2017

81. Infinite Hope (www.infinitehope.org) / infinitehopeanimalrescue@gmail.com

82. Phillip Mlynar, '6 Greatest Guinness World Records Starring Cats,' CatTime.com

83. Photo by Regina Carrone, Catopia Cat Rescue Director (catopiacatrescue.org) / catopiacatrescue@gmail.com

84. 'Why cats lose their minds over this perennial herb' (www.humanesociety.org/resources/crazy-catnip)

85. Infinite Hope (www.infinitehope.org) / infinitehopeanimalrescue@gmail.com

86. Judy Molland, '5 Reasons You Should Never Share Your Bed With Your Cat,' Care2.com, February 12 2017

87. Photo by Emilie Chiang, Give Me Shelter Volunteer (www.givemesheltersf.org) / info@givemesheltersf.org

88. Stephanie Pappas, 'Feline Find: How the Tabby Cat Got Its Stripes,' LiveScience.com, September 20 2012

89. Bobbi and the Strays Pet Rescue (www.bobbiandthestrays.org) / info@bobbicares.org

90. Kaitlin Stainbrook, '8 Hair-Raising Facts About Black Cats,' MentalFloss.com, August 17 2018 // 'Bombay Cat' (https://www.purina.com/cats/cat-breeds/bombay)

91. Photo by Regina Carrone, Catopia Cat Rescue Director (catopiacatrescue.org) / catopiacatrescue@gmail.com

92. Betty Lewis, 'How Is It Possible That Kittens Have More Than One Father?' Pets.TheNest.com

93. Photo by Regina Carrone, Catopia Cat Rescue Director (catopiacatrescue.org) / catopiacatrescue@gmail.com

94. Steve Duno, '12 Sounds Cats Make and What They Mean,' ModernCat.com

95. Photo by Kelly Parker, Chicago Cat Rescue Volunteer Photographer (www.chicagocatrescue.org/) / (773) 203-0215

96. Lynne Tuohy, 'Now a Jailbird, Lewis the Cat awaits his Fate,' Courant.com, June 20 2006 // 'Purrfect ending to story of the felonious feline,' NYDailynews.com, July 5 2008

97. Photo by Regina Carrone, Catopia Cat Rescue Director (catopiacatrescue.org) / catopiacatrescue@gmail.com

98. 'Secrets of Animal Acrobats: Why Are Cats So Flexible?' CatCheckup.com, January 30 2019

99. Photo by Regina Carrone, Catopia Cat Rescue Director (catopiacatrescue.org) / catopiacatrescue@gmail.com

100. American Pet Products Association (www.americanpetproducts.org/press_industrytrends.asp)

101/102. Photo by Regina Carrone, Catopia Cat Rescue Director (catopiacatrescue.org) / catopiacatrescue@gmail.com. BACKGROUND: Vitani, the cat pictured, was not rescued from a shark attack; rather she was discovered in a Florida parking lot with a severe leg injury. Vitani's leg was amputated due to the extent of the injury. Thanks to the efforts of Catopia Cat Rescue, Vitani has since been placed in a loving forever home that includes two other tripod (three-legged) cats, one tripod dog, and a special needs dog. In the words of Catopia Director Regina Carrone, "She ended up in the perfect home and is deeply loved."

ABOUT THE AUTHOR

Michael D. Mullins is an award-winning journalist, lifelong animal lover, cat rescuer, and U.S. Marine veteran. He publishes the animal news website 4PawNews.com and is the former publisher of the animal welfare newspaper— *The New York Companion*. A proud NYC native, Michael now resides in upstate NY with his beautiful wife and two amazing, animal-loving sons. The author attributes all his accomplishments to the guidance, sacrifice, and love given by his parents, Timothy Mullins and Theresa Cummings, and his grandmother, Rose Marsico-Cummings.